GRAPHIC AMERICA

WESTWARD, HO!

DARREN SECHRIST

I0809750

Crabtree Publishing
crabtreebooks.com

Crabtree Publishing

crabtreebooks.com 800-387-7650

Hardcover 978-0-7787-4190-9
Paperback 978-0-7787-4217-3
Ebook (pdf) 978-0-7787-8959-8

Printed in Canada
042024/CP20240423

Library and Archives Canada Cataloguing in Publication

Sechrist, Darren
Westward, ho! / Darren Sechrist.

(Graphic America)
Includes index.
ISBN 978-0-7787-4190-9 (bound).--
ISBN 978-0-7787-4217-3 (pbk.)

1. Frontier and pioneer life--West (U.S.)--Comic books, strips, etc.--Juvenile literature. 2. Pioneers--West (U.S.)--History--19th century--Comic books, strips, etc.--Juvenile literature. 3. Overland journeys to the Pacific--Comic books, strips, etc.--Juvenile literature. 4. West (U.S.)--History--19th century--Comic books, strips, etc.--Juvenile literature. 5. United States--Territorial expansion--Comic books, strips, etc.--Juvenile literature. I. Title. II. Series.

F596.S423 2008 8'.02 C2008-906

Published in Canada
Crabtree Publishing
616 Welland Avenue
St. Catharines, Ontario
L2M 5V6

Published in the United States
Crabtree Publishing
347 Fifth Avenue
Suite 1402-145
New York, NY 10016

Author: Darren Sechrist
Coordinating editor: Chester Fisher
Editors: Scholastic Ventures Inc., Molly Aloian
Copy editor: Scholastic Ventures Inc.
Proofreaders: Adrianna Morganelli, Crystal Sikkens
Project editor: Robert Walker
Production coordinator: Margaret Amy Salter
Prepress technicians: Ken Wright, Margaret Amy Salter
Logo design: Samantha Crabtree
Project manager: Santosh Vasudevan (Q2AMedia)
Art direction: Rahul Dhiman (Q2AMedia)
Design: Tarang Saggar (Q2AMedia)
Illustrations: Q2AMedia

Library of Congress Cataloging-in-Publication Data

Sechrist, Darren.
Westward, ho! / Darren Sechrist.
p. cm. -- (Graphic America)
Includes index.
ISBN-13: 978-0-7787-4217-3 (pbk. : alk. paper)
ISBN-10: 0-7787-4217-2 (pbk. : alk. paper)
ISBN-13: 978-0-7787-4190-9 (reinforced library binding : alk. paper)
ISBN-10: 0-7787-4190-7 (reinforced library binding : alk. paper)
1. rontier and pioneer life--West (U.S.)--Comic books, strips, etc.--Juvenile literature. 2. Pioneers--West (U.S.)--History--19th century--Comic books, strips, etc.--Juvenile literature. 3. Overland journeys to the Pacific--Comic books, strips, etc.--Juvenile literature. 4. West (U.S.)--History--19th century--Comic books, strips, etc.--Juvenile literature. 5. United States--Territorial expansion--Comic books, strips, etc.--Juvenile literature. 6. Graphic novels. I. Title. II. Series.

F596.S33 2009
978'.02--dc22

2008041857

CONTENTS

THE GROWTH OF A NATION

IT'S AGREED THEN. THE UNITED STATES WILL TAKE POSSESSION OF THESE LANDS FOR THE PRICE OF $15 MILLION.

*IN THE EARLY 1800S, THE UNITED STATES WAS A VERY SMALL NATION. IN 1803, U.S. PRESIDENT THOMAS JEFFERSON WAS WORKING TO HELP THE COUNTRY GROW. HE SENT JAMES MONROE TO MEET WITH FRENCH LEADER NAPOLEON BONAPARTE. THE U.S. AND FRANCE QUICKLY AGREED ON THE LOUISIANA PURCHASE. IT ADDED 828,000 SQUARE MILES (2,144,520 SQUARE KILOMETERS) TO THE YOUNG COUNTRY'S **TERRITORY**.*

WHAT DID HE SAY?
THE CHIEF HAS AGREED TO PROVIDE US WITH THE FOOD AND HORSES WE NEED TO CONTINUE OUR **JOURNEY**.

*IN 1804, PRESIDENT JEFFERSON SENT MERIWETHER LEWIS AND WILLIAM CLARK ON A TASK. HE WANTED THEM TO TRAVEL AROUND THE NEW LANDS. LEWIS AND CLARK'S **CORPS** OF DISCOVERY MADE THE HARD JOURNEY THROUGH LOUISIANA. A NATIVE AMERICAN WOMAN NAMED SACAGAWEA WAS THEIR GUIDE. THEY RETURNED MORE THAN TWO YEARS LATER. THEY CREATED MAPS OF THE NEW LANDS.*

AS THE UNITED STATES GREW, FEW PEOPLE WENT WEST OF THE MISSISSIPPI RIVER. THIS LAND WAS CALLED THE "GREAT AMERICAN DESERT." PEOPLE WANTED TO REMAIN IN THE EAST. SOME STAYED ON THEIR FAMILY FARMS, OTHERS CONTINUED TO LIVE IN CITIES LIKE NEW YORK, PHILADELPHIA, AND BOSTON.
FRESH FISH FOR SALE! FRESH FISH!

WE'VE HAD A GOOD DAY—MANY ANIMAL FURS AND A GOOD SUPPLY OF MEAT AS WELL.
FROM THE EARLY 1800S THROUGH THE 1830S, ONLY A FEW BRAVE SOULS MADE THEIR WAY WEST. MANY WERE HUNTERS WHO SOLD THEIR GOODS TO EUROPEAN TRADERS. THEY LIVED IN SMALL SETTLEMENTS, AMONG THE **NATIVE AMERICANS** THAT ROAMED THE GREAT **PLAINS**. LITTLE DID THESE HUNTERS AND TRADERS KNOW THAT THEY WOULD SOON BE JOINED BY THOUSANDS OF AMERICANS, SEEKING THEIR FORTUNE IN THIS WILD LAND.

EARLY SETTLEMENT IN TEXAS

ONE OF THE FEW PLACES BEING SETTLED BY AMERICANS WAS TEXAS. AMERICAN COWBOYS USED THE OPEN COUNTRYSIDE TO RAISE CATTLE. BUT IN THE EARLY 1800S, TEXAS WAS UNDER THE CONTROL OF SPAIN. TO KEEP THE PEACE, AMERICAN MOSES AUSTIN ARRANGED TO START A U.S. **COLONY** IN TEXAS.
HIYAAH! MOVE ALONG, DOGGIE!

WITH A BIT MORE WORK, WE'LL HAVE FINISHED OUR HOME.
WHEN MEXICO GAINED ITS FREEDOM FROM SPAIN IN 1821, IT TOOK CONTROL OF TEXAS. AFTER AUSTIN'S DEATH, HIS SON STEPHEN F. AUSTIN WORKED TO KEEP THE COLONY. AUSTIN LATER HELPED TO BRING IN HUNDREDS OF AMERICAN FAMILIES.

THE YOUNG COLONY GREW QUICKLY. BY THE MID-1830S, THERE WERE MORE THAN 20,000 AMERICANS LIVING IN TEXAS. THERE WERE ONLY ABOUT 3,500 MEXICANS IN THE SAME AREA. MANY AMERICANS DID NOT LIKE LIVING UNDER MEXICAN RULE. **SETTLERS** OFTEN FOUGHT AGAINST THE MEXICAN **MILITARY**.

BUT WHAT ARE THE CHARGES AGAINST ME? WHAT HAVE I DONE?

STEPHEN AUSTIN SAW THAT HE NEEDED TO REACH PEACE WITH MEXICO IN ORDER TO KEEP HIS COLONY ALIVE. IN 1833, HE WENT TO MEXICO CITY AND PROPOSED THAT TEXAS BECOME A MEXICAN STATE. BUT THE MEXICANS REFUSED. ON THE WAY BACK TO TEXAS, AUSTIN WAS ARRESTED. THE MEXICAN GOVERNMENT HAD FEARED THAT HE WOULD LEAD A **REVOLT**.

REMEMBER THE ALAMO

AUSTIN RETURNED TO TEXAS IN 1835 A CHANGED MAN. HE WAS NO LONGER SET ON KEEPING PEACE WITH MEXICO. HE QUICKLY JOINED AN **INDEPENDENCE** EFFORT LED BY SAMUEL HOUSTON.
WE ARE THE MAJORITY IN TEXAS. WHY SHOULD WE BE RULED BY THE LAWS OF MEXICO?
WE MUST DEFEND OUR LANDS!

THE TEXAN FIGHTERS ATTACKED MEXICAN-HELD SAN ANTONIO AND TOOK IT OVER. MEXICO'S PRESIDENT ANTONIO LÓPEZ DE SANTA ANNA SENT IN THE MEXICAN ARMY.

WE MAY DIE HERE TODAY. BUT WE MUST FIGHT FOR OUR FREEDOM!

THOUSANDS OF MEXICAN SOLDIERS SOON ARRIVED IN SAN ANTONIO. IN MARCH 1836, THEY ATTACKED AN OLD CHURCH KNOWN AS THE ALAMO, WITH 180 TEXANS INSIDE. THE TEXAN LEADER, WILLIAM B. TRAVIS, REFUSED TO GIVE UP. THE MEXICANS STORMED THE CHURCH AND KILLED ALL OF THE TEXANS INSIDE. AMONG THE DEAD WERE AMERICAN **FRONTIERSMEN** JAMES BOWIE AND DAVY CROCKETT.

THE TEXANS LOST THE BATTLE AT THE ALAMO, BUT THEY WERE NOT DEFEATED. HOUSTON USED THE STORY OF THE ALAMO TO STIR UP HIS SOLDIERS. HE LED 900 MEN INTO BATTLE AGAINST THE MEXICAN ARMY AT SAN JACINTO. THE TEXANS WON THE BATTLE AND GAINED FREEDOM FOR TEXAS. NINE YEARS LATER, TEXAS BECAME PART OF THE UNITED STATES.
REMEMBER THE ALAMO!

WAR WITH MEXICO

WE WOULD BE WILLING TO OFFER MORE THAN $25 MILLION IN RETURN FOR THAT SOUTHERN PORTION OF TEXAS.
THAT LAND BELONGS TO MEXICO. IT IS NOT FOR SALE.

WHEN TEXAS BECAME PART OF THE UNITED STATES IN 1845, MEXICO BROKE OFF CONTACT WITH ITS NEIGHBOR TO THE NORTH. MORE TROUBLE AROSE WHEN THE UNITED STATES SAID THAT LAND ALL THE WAY SOUTH TO THE RIO GRANDE RIVER WAS PART OF TEXAS. U.S. PRESIDENT JAMES K. POLK SENT ***CONGRESSMAN*** *JOHN SLIDELL TO MEXICO TO TRY TO BUY THE LAND, BUT MEXICO DID NOT WANT TO SELL IT.*

THIS WHOLE WAR IS UNJUST—I WON'T BE A PART OF IT.
IF WE SERVE, WE CAN STOP THE MEXICANS, AND BE REWARDED WITH LARGE PLOTS OF LAND.
CO.
WITH HIS OFFER REJECTED, POLK WAS NOT ABOUT TO BACK DOWN. IN 1846, HE SENT U.S. SOLDIERS TO THE BORDER ALONG THE RIO GRANDE. IN LATE APRIL, MEXICO ATTACKED THE U.S. SOLDIERS. ON MAY 13, THE MEXICAN-AMERICAN WAR BEGAN. MANY AMERICANS EAGERLY SIGNED UP TO FIGHT FOR THEIR COUNTRY. OTHERS THOUGHT POLK STARTED THE WAR JUST TO GET LAND.

GENERAL ZACHARY TAYLOR, KNOWN AS OLD ROUGH AND READY, LED THE U.S. SOLDIERS IN TEXAS. TAYLOR WON KEY BATTLES AT THE BORDER. HE THEN LED HIS MEN INTO MEXICO, WHERE HE WAS OFTEN ABLE TO WIN WITH FEWER SOLDIERS THAN THE MEXICANS HAD.

I **PROCLAIM** THIS THE REPUBLIC OF CALIFORNIA.
TROUBLE WAS ALSO STARTING IN CALIFORNIA. AMERICAN EXPLORER JOHN C. FREMONT LED A GROUP OF AMERICANS AGAINST THE MEXICAN GOVERNMENT. IT WAS CALLED THE BEAR FLAG REVOLT. IN JUNE, THEY TOOK OVER THE CITY OF SONOMA AND MADE IT PART OF THE REPUBLIC OF CALIFORNIA. FREMONT WAS MADE THE PRESIDENT OF THE YOUNG NATION.

THE WAR BETWEEN THE UNITED STATES AND MEXICO SOON SPREAD WEST. GENERAL STEPHEN W. KEARNY TOOK OVER THE CITY OF SANTA FE. HE THEN QUICKLY TOOK CONTROL OF NEW MEXICO. UNITED STATES SOLDIERS MOVED ON TO TAKE CALIFORNIA IN 1847. THE U.S. NAVY HELPED SUPPORT THE ARMY'S SOLDIERS. THE SHORT-LIVED REPUBLIC OF CALIFORNIA GAVE WAY TO U.S. CONTROL.

PUSH THEM BACK INTO THE CENTRAL SQUARE AND WE CAN TAKE THE CITY!
AFTER DEFEATING MEXICAN SOLDIERS AT THE BORDER, TAYLOR LED HIS ARMY INTO MEXICO. THEY ATTACKED MONTERREY IN SEPTEMBER 1846 AND FOUGHT BATTLES IN THE CITY'S STREETS. MANY SOLDIERS ON BOTH SIDES LOST THEIR LIVES, BUT THE AMERICANS EVENTUALLY WON. VICTORIES AT BUENA VISTA AND VERACRUZ FOLLOWED.

THE U.S. ARMY ATTACKED THE CAPITAL, MEXICO CITY, IN THE LAST BATTLE OF THE WAR. ON SEPTEMBER 13, 1847, THE AMERICANS STORMED CHAPULTEPEC PALACE. THE LAST LINE OF DEFENSE WAS A GROUP OF YOUNG SOLDIERS FROM MEXICO'S MILITARY SCHOOL. THEY COULD NOT HOLD OFF THE AMERICAN TROOPS. MEXICO SURRENDERED ON SEPTEMBER 17.
WE TAKE THIS CITY IN THE NAME OF THE UNITED STATES GOVERNMENT.
THE **TREATY** OF GUADALUPE HIDALGO WAS AN AGREEMENT THAT ENDED THE WAR ON FEBRUARY 2, 1848. MEXICO AGREED TO GIVE A HUGE AMOUNT OF LAND TO THE UNITED STATES. IT INCLUDED CALIFORNIA, UTAH, NEVADA, AND MOST OF ARIZONA AND NEW MEXICO. MANY AMERICANS WERE HAPPY WITH THE WAR. OTHERS, HOWEVER, FELT THAT THEIR COUNTRY HAD BEEN WRONG TO ATTACK MEXICO.
WE'VE DEFEATED MEXICO. CALIFORNIA IS OURS!
VICTORY
VICTORY

A WHOLE NEW WORLD

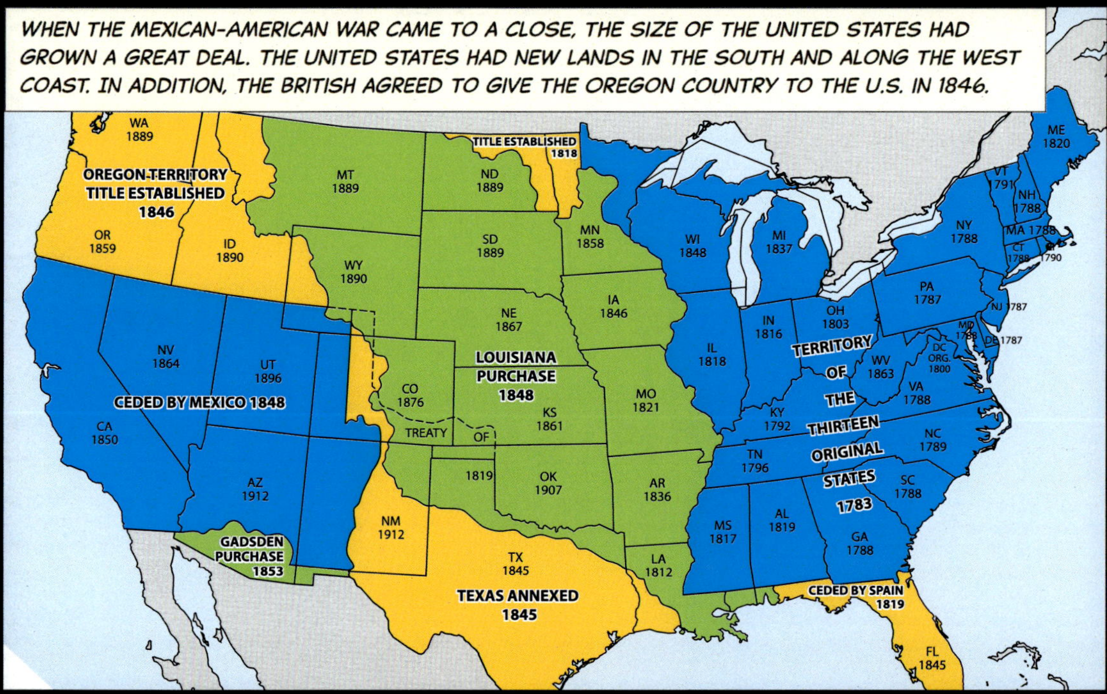

SEE? THE BLADE CUTS THROUGH THE SOIL LIKE BUTTER.
THE FLAT LANDS OF THE MIDWEST AND WEST WERE COVERED WITH HEAVY SOILS THAT WERE HARD TO DIG UP. IN THE 1830S, BLACKSMITH JOHN DEERE MADE A NEW PLOW THAT WORKED BETTER. IT WAS STRONGER THAN OTHER PLOWS, AND ITS STEEL BLADE EASILY CUT THROUGH THE DIRT.

IN THE LATE 1830S, A NEW WAY OF SENDING MESSAGES WAS INVENTED. USING A TELEGRAPH MACHINE, PEOPLE COULD SEND SOUNDS AS DASHES AND DOTS TO EACH OTHER. THESE SOUNDS WERE TURNED BACK INTO WORDS USING MORSE CODE, WHICH WAS CREATED BY SAMUEL MORSE. THIS ALLOWED PEOPLE TO QUICKLY SEND MESSAGES ACROSS THE COUNTRY.
HE SAYS THAT THEY MADE IT TO THEIR **DESTINATION** SAFELY!

TRAILS TO THE WEST

WITH HUGE AMOUNTS OF LAND READY TO BE FARMED, THE WIDE OPEN LANDS OF THE WEST DREW MORE AND MORE AMERICANS. MANY FAMILIES PACKED THEIR THINGS, THREW CAUTION TO THE WIND, AND SET OUT FOR A NEW LIFE.
BUT PAPA, I'M SCARED.
IT WILL BE A WHOLE NEW LIFE FOR US. YOU'LL SEE.

WE MUST WORK TOGETHER TO ASSURE THAT WE ALL HAVE A SAFE PASSAGE.
GETTING TO THE WEST COAST WAS NOT EASY. FAMILIES BANDED TOGETHER AND FORMED WAGON TRAINS THAT MOVED AS A GROUP. BETWEEN THE 1820S AND 1840S, MANY WAGON TRAINS TRAVELED THE SANTA FE TRAIL TO NEW MEXICO. TRAILS TO OREGON AND CALIFORNIA FOLLOWED.
HELP YOUR FELLOW MAN AND YOU WILL BE HELPING YOURSELF.

CIRCLE THE WAGONS. WE'RE UNDER ATTACK!

LIFE ON THE TRAIL WAS VERY HARD. JOURNEYS ACROSS THE COUNTRY COULD TAKE SEVERAL MONTHS. ALONG THE WAY, THE SETTLERS BATTLED FREEZING WINTERS AND DRY SUMMERS. THEY WERE SOMETIMES ATTACKED BY NATIVE AMERICANS WHO WERE TRYING TO PROTECT THEIR TRADITIONAL TERRITORIES.

MOST OF THE WAGON TRAINS FINISHED THEIR JOURNEYS. BUT SOME MET WITH TRAGEDY. THE DONNER PARTY IS THE MOST FAMOUS EXAMPLE. IN 1846, THE GROUP OF 87 SET OUT FROM ILLINOIS FOR CALIFORNIA. THEY FOLLOWED A ROUTE NO ONE HAD USED BEFORE. THEY BECAME TRAPPED BY HEAVY SNOW IN THE SIERRA NEVADA MOUNTAINS. ONLY 47 PEOPLE SURVIVED.

I CAN'T SEE THE TRAIL.
KEEP PRESSING FORWARD. WE'RE DOOMED IF WE STAY HERE!

THROUGH THIS BOOK, I CAN TEACH YOU ABOUT THE ONE TRUE GOD.
OREGON WAS AN EARLY DRAW IN THE WEST. CHRISTIANS FIRST ARRIVED IN THE 1830S. THEY SET UP A CHURCH HOPING TO SPREAD THEIR RELIGION TO THE CAYUSE AND OTHER NATIVE NATIONS. BUT THE NATIVE AMERICANS WANTED TO KEEP THEIR TRADITIONAL WAYS, AND THE CHURCH CLOSED IN 1842.

SETTLERS ARRIVED IN OREGON LITTLE BY LITTLE. IN 1843, ONE OF THE OREGON **MISSIONARIES**, A DOCTOR NAMED MARCUS WHITMAN, RETURNED EAST TO HELP GUIDE A GROUP OF MORE THAN 1,000 SETTLERS ALONG THE TRAIL FROM MISSOURI TO OREGON.
MOTHER, I'M TIRED.
KEEP WALKING, DEAR. WE'LL STOP SOON AND COOK OUR DINNER. THEN YOU CAN REST AND I'LL TELL YOU A STORY.

IT IS JUST AS BEAUTIFUL AS THEY SAID IT WOULD BE.
WE WILL CERTAINLY HAVE A BOUNTIFUL CROP THIS YEAR.
AFTER FIVE MONTHS, WHITMAN'S PARTY REACHED THE END OF THEIR JOURNEY. THEY QUICKLY STARTED CLAIMING PIECES OF LAND AND SETTING UP FARMS. WHITMAN WAS NOT SO LUCKY. HE WAS KILLED BY CAYUSE INDIANS IN 1847.

WHERE ARE YOU HEADED TO?
WE ARE BOUND FOR THE OPEN FIELDS OF OREGON.
THIS GREAT **MIGRATION** WAS THE BEGINNING OF OREGON FEVER. IT WAS A HUGE MOVEMENT OF PEOPLE SEARCHING FOR GOOD FARMLAND. BY 1848, AROUND 5,000 SETTLERS HAD MADE THEIR WAY TO OREGON. THAT NUMBER GREW INTO THE 1860S.

THE MORMONS MOVE WEST

I WAS INFORMED THAT I WAS CHOSEN TO BE AN INSTRUMENT IN THE HANDS OF GOD TO BRING ABOUT SOME OF HIS PURPOSES IN THIS GLORIOUS **DISPENSATION**.*
GREAT FARMING WAS NOT THE ONLY REASON PEOPLE MOVED WEST. A RELIGIOUS GROUP IN NEW YORK KNOWN AS THE MORMONS DID SO TO ESCAPE ATTACKS FROM PEOPLE WHO DISAGREED WITH THEM. THEIR LEADER AND FOUNDER, JOSEPH SMITH, SAID HE HAD BEEN VISITED BY AN ANGEL. HIS SPEECHES QUICKLY DREW HIM THOUSANDS OF FOLLOWERS.

BUT SOME WERE UPSET WITH SMITH. THEY THOUGHT THAT HIS TEACHINGS WENT AGAINST WHAT OTHER CHRISTIANS BELIEVED. SMITH HAD TO MOVE HIS FOLLOWERS TO OHIO, MISSOURI, AND THEN ILLINOIS.
THEY SAY THAT WE WILL FIND A PLACE TO PRACTICE OUR BELIEFS FREELY IN ILLINOIS.
I HOPE THEY ARE RIGHT.

*ACTUAL QUOTE

BUT SMITH AND HIS FOLLOWERS DID NOT FIND PEACE IN NAUVOO, ILLINOIS. THEY FOUGHT WITH NON-MORMONS. IN 1844, SMITH WAS SENT TO JAIL FOR DESTROYING A LOCAL NEWSPAPER'S PRESS. WHILE HE WAS THERE, A GROUP OF ANGRY PEOPLE ARRIVED AND SHOT HIM TO DEATH.
WE ARE GOING TO GET YOU, SMITH!
THREE YEARS LATER, UNDER THE LEADERSHIP OF BRIGHAM YOUNG, THE MORMONS MOVED ON TO WHAT IS NOW UTAH. THERE, THEY WERE ABLE TO PRACTICE THEIR RELIGION IN PEACE. THEIR NUMBERS GREW QUICKLY, AND BY THE 1870S, MORE THAN 170,000 MORMONS LIVED THERE.

CALIFORNIA AND THE GOLD RUSH

AMERICANS STARTED HEADING FOR CALIFORNIA AS EARLY AS THE 1820S, AFTER A ROUTE HAD BEEN MAPPED OUT BY A **TRAPPER** NAMED JEDEDIAH SMITH. BY THE 1840S, THE NUMBERS OF AMERICANS HAD ONLY REACHED A FEW HUNDRED. MANY OF THEM WORKED AT RANCHING AND TRADED WITH AMERICAN SHIPS AND SHIPS FROM OTHER COUNTRIES.
I HAVE HUNDREDS OF HIDES TO TRADE—WHAT HAVE YOU GOT TO OFFER?
WE HAVE FOOD, FARMING TOOLS, AND MANY OTHER THINGS THAT WILL SUIT YOUR NEEDS.

OH MY...IT CAN'T BE... BUT IT IS...GOLD!
ON JANUARY 24, 1848, AMERICAN JAMES MARSHALL MADE A DISCOVERY THAT WOULD CHANGE THE WEST FOREVER. WHILE WORKING AT JOHN SUTTER'S MILL NEAR SACRAMENTO, HE NOTICED SOMETHING SPARKLING IN THE AMERICAN RIVER. HE HAD DISCOVERED GOLD!

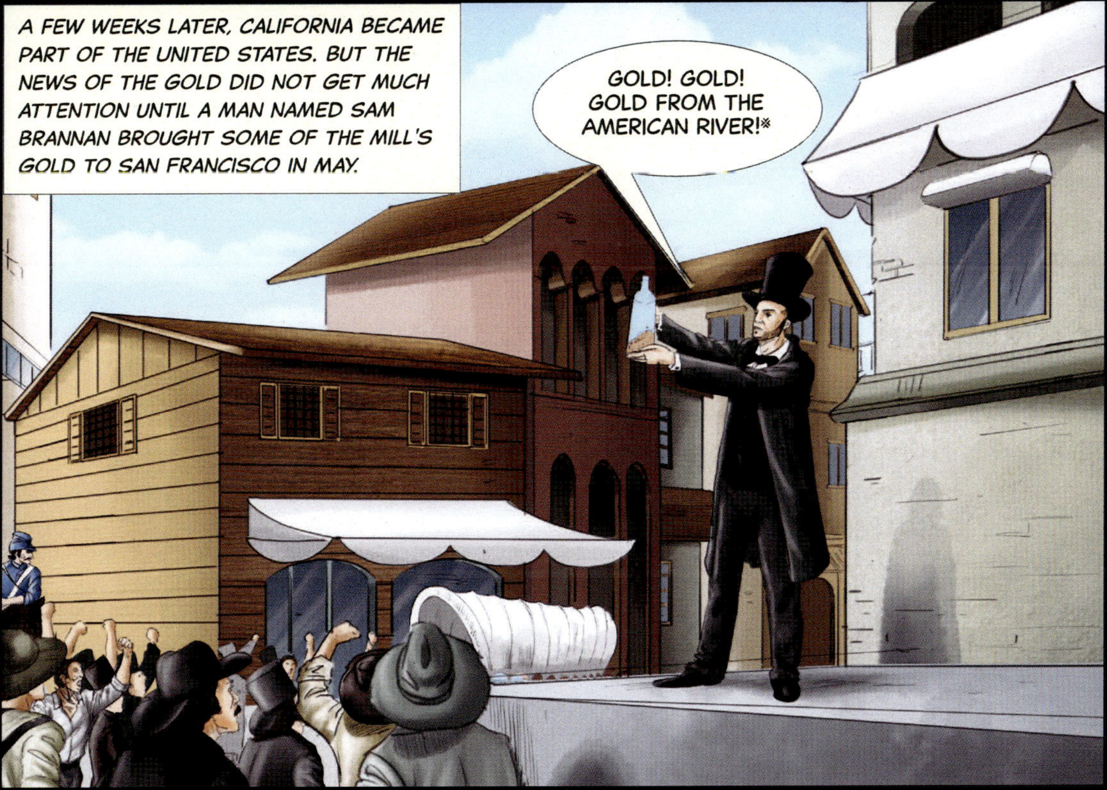
A FEW WEEKS LATER, CALIFORNIA BECAME PART OF THE UNITED STATES. BUT THE NEWS OF THE GOLD DID NOT GET MUCH ATTENTION UNTIL A MAN NAMED SAM BRANNAN BROUGHT SOME OF THE MILL'S GOLD TO SAN FRANCISCO IN MAY.
GOLD! GOLD! GOLD FROM THE AMERICAN RIVER!※

PEOPLE FROM ALL WALKS OF LIFE DROPPED EVERYTHING AND RUSHED TO THE AREA OF SUTTER'S MILL IN HOPES OF GETTING RICH. SOON, SAN FRANCISCO WAS ALMOST LIKE A **GHOST TOWN**, WITH MANY OF ITS HOMES DESERTED AND ITS BUSINESSES CLOSED.
EVERY DAY ANOTHER MAN STRIKES IT RICH OUT THERE...AND ONE DAY IT WILL BE ME.

※ACTUAL QUOTE

CLIPPER
IT DID NOT TAKE LONG FOR NEWS OF GOLD TO REACH THE REST OF THE COUNTRY. BY 1849, THOUSANDS OF AMERICANS WERE STREAMING WEST. THE CALIFORNIA GOLD RUSH HAD BEGUN. SOME OF THE FIRST PEOPLE HEADED WEST ON A DIFFICULT FIVE-MONTH SEA JOURNEY AROUND CAPE HORN IN SOUTH AMERICA.

BUT MOST **FORTY-NINERS**, AS THEY WERE CALLED, MADE THE JOURNEY OVER LAND. THEY ARRIVED IN CALIFORNIA, READY TO FIND THEIR FORTUNE. THEY SET ABOUT **PANNING** RIVERS FOR GOLD. WHEN THEY FOUND GOLD, THEY STAKED THEIR CLAIM, MARKING THE SPOT AS THEIRS AND THEIRS ALONE.
SEE? RIGHT THERE, THAT'S GOLD.

FORTY-NINERS LIVED HARD LIVES. THEY SPENT THEIR NIGHTS IN TENTS AND THEIR DAYS KNEE-DEEP IN FREEZING WATER. TERRIBLE FIGHTS OFTEN BROKE OUT. TO MAKE MATTERS WORSE, MANY HAD COME WEST WITH NO IDEA HOW TO LIVE OUTDOORS.
OUR SUPPLIES ARE RUNNING SHORT. WE HAD BETTER FIND SOMETHING SOON.

OVER THE NEXT FEW YEARS, SOME MINERS DID FIND GOLD. THEY DISCOVERED TENS OF MILLIONS OF DOLLARS WORTH EACH YEAR. BUT BY THE MID-1850S, MOST OF THE BEST SPOTS FOR MINING HAD BEEN TAKEN. BY THEN, THE SAN FRANCISCO AREA HAD GREATLY CHANGED. ONCE A SMALL TOWN IN THE WEST, IT WAS NOW A BUSY CITY. BY THE 1860S, MORE THAN 300,000 HAD FOUND THEIR WAY TO CALIFORNIA.
I SAY, THE CITY HAS GROWN SO QUICKLY THAT I SCARCELY RECOGNIZE IT FROM DAY TO DAY.

MORE RUSHES FOR PRECIOUS METALS

SOON AFTER THE CALIFORNIA GOLD RUSH DIED DOWN, THE COMSTOCK LODE WAS DISCOVERED AT MT. DAVIDSON IN NEVADA. FROM 1859 TO 1882, MINERS FOUND MORE THAN $400 MILLION WORTH OF SILVER.
WE'VE FILLED ANOTHER CART. I'LL BE BACK WITH ANOTHER.

ALSO IN 1859, GOLD WAS DISCOVERED AT PIKE'S PEAK IN CLEAR CREEK, COLORADO. BY THE YEAR'S END, MORE THAN 100,000 PEOPLE HAD RUSHED TO THE SITE. SOON AFTER, THE CITY OF DENVER WAS FOUNDED.
SO, THIS WILL BE OUR NEW HOME?
THIS LAND WILL MAKE US RICH. I CAN FEEL IT.
PIKE'S PEAK OR BUST

OTHER RUSHES FOLLOWED IN IDAHO, MONTANA, AND THE DAKOTAS. THE WEST WAS QUICKLY FILLED WITH NEW SETTLERS OF ALL KINDS. CITIES WERE QUICKLY BUILT UP WITH BUSINESSPEOPLE, TRADERS, AND OTHERS.

GIVE ME EVERYTHING YOU'VE GOT. DON'T HOLD BACK A PENNY!
BUT THERE WAS VERY LITTLE GOVERNMENT IN THESE NEW LANDS, AND LAW AND ORDER WAS HARD TO FIND. THE TIME OF THE **WILD WEST** WAS JUST BEGINNING.

TIMELINE

1803 – THE UNITED STATES PURCHASES 828,000 SQUARE MILES OF LAND FROM FRANCE IN THE LOUISIANA PURCHASE.

1804–1806 – WITH THE HELP OF SACAGAWEA, LEWIS AND CLARK'S CORPS OF DISCOVERY EXPLORES THE AMERICAN WEST.

1821 – MEXICO WINS ITS INDEPENDENCE FROM SPAIN AND TAKES CONTROL OF TEXAS.

1836 – IN MARCH, MEXICO DEFEATS THE TEXANS IN THE BATTLE OF THE ALAMO; SIX WEEKS LATER, SAMUEL HOUSTON LEADS A GROUP OF TEXANS WHO DEFEAT MEXICO IN SAN JACINTO.

1845 – TEXAS BECOMES A PART OF THE UNITED STATES.

1846 — THE MEXICAN-AMERICAN WAR BREAKS OUT. IT ENDS TWO YEARS LATER WITH THE UNITED STATES RECEIVING THE LAND THAT WILL LATER BE THE STATES OF CALIFORNIA, UTAH, NEVADA, AND MOST OF ARIZONA AND NEW MEXICO.

1847 — BRIGHAM YOUNG LEADS THE MORMONS INTO UTAH WHERE THEY FINALLY FIND A PERMANENT HOME.

1848 — GOLD IS DISCOVERED IN CALIFORNIA, LEADING TO A RUSH OF SETTLERS LOOKING TO STRIKE IT RICH.

1859 — THE COMSTOCK LODE, A HUGE SILVER SUPPLY, BEGINS DRAWING SETTLERS TO NEVADA; GOLD IS ALSO DISCOVERED IN COLORADO.

GLOSSARY

COLONY A GROUP OF PEOPLE LIVING IN A NEWLY SETTLED AREA BUT UNDER THE CONTROL OF ANOTHER GOVERNMENT

CONGRESSMAN A MEMBER OF THE BRANCH OF U.S. GOVERNMENT THAT MAKES LAWS

CORPS A GROUP OF PEOPLE WORKING TOGETHER TO COMPLETE A TASK

DESTINATION THE PLACE AT THE END OF A PERSON'S TRIP

DISPENSATION A HOLY ORDER PREVAILING AT A PARTICULAR TIME IN HISTORY

FORTY-NINER A PERSON WHO TRAVELED TO CALIFORNIA IN THE MID-1800S, LOOKING FOR GOLD

FRONTIERSMEN PEOPLE WHO LIVE ON THE EDGES OF SETTLED OR DEVELOPED LANDS

GENERAL A HIGH-RANKING OFFICER

GHOST TOWN A TOWN THAT HAS BEEN LEFT EMPTY

INDEPENDENCE BEING FREE FROM THE CONTROL OF OTHERS

JOURNEY A LONG AND SOMETIMES DIFFICULT TRIP

MIGRATION THE MOVEMENT OF PEOPLE FROM ONE PLACE TO ANOTHER

MILITARY THE ARMED FORCES (SUCH AS THE ARMY AND NAVY) OF A NATION

MISSIONARY A PERSON WHO WORKS TO SPREAD HIS OR HER RELIGION TO NEW FOLLOWERS

NATIVE AMERICAN ANY OF THE GROUPS OF PEOPLES WHO LIVED IN THE AMERICAS BEFORE THE ARRIVAL OF EUROPEANS. THEY ARE ALSO CALLED "INDIANS"

PANNING USING A PAN TO SIFT THROUGH WATER AND GRAVEL TO FIND GOLD

PLAINS LARGE LEVEL AREAS OF TREELESS LAND

PROCLAIM ANNOUNCE SOMETHING OFFICIALLY

REAPING CUTTING WHEAT OR OTHER PLANTS TO HARVEST THEM

REVOLT TO RISE UP AGAINST SOMETHING OR SOMEONE

SETTLER A PERSON WHO MOVES INTO A NEW AREA OR REGION

TERRITORY AN AREA OF LAND UNDER THE CONTROL OF A GOVERNMENT

TRAPPER A PERSON WHO TRAPS ANIMALS FOR FUR AND/OR FOOD

TREATY A FORMAL AGREEMENT BETWEEN TWO GROUPS OR NATIONS

INDEX

WEBFINDER

HTTP://WWW.AMERICANWEST.COM/
HTTP://WWW.PBS.ORG/LEWISANDCLARK/
HTTP://WWW.NATIONALGEOGRAPHIC.COM/LEWISANDCLARK/
HTTP://PBSKIDS.ORG/WAYBACK/GOLDRUSH/INDEX.HTML
HTTP://WWW.ISU.EDU/~TRINMICH/OREGONTRAIL.HTML
HTTP://WWW.PBS.ORG/WETA/THEWEST/PROGRAM/
HTTP://WWW.MTMEN.ORG/

GRAPHIC AMERICA
FREE
AT LAST!
OW THE FREEING OF THE SLAVES CHANGED AMERICAN HISTORY